M000234598

THE GREAT BOOK OF

yorkshire pudding

ELAINE LEMM

GREAT NORTHERN

Great Northern Books
PO Box 213, Ilkley, LS29 9WS
www.greatnorthernbooks.co.uk

ISBN: 978 1 905080 80 9

Design and layout: David Burrill
Photographs by Ron Blenkinsop

CIP Data
A catalogue for this book is available from the British Library

Acknowledgments

Thank you first and foremost to all those who through the years have kept the tradition of the Yorkshire pudding alive; without it our culinary heritage would be the poorer. To everyone who shared stories, tales and memories of Yorkshire puddings, a big thank you, hearing them all made the writing of the book so much fun.

Special thanks to my wonderful parents who taught me the joy of food and cooking in making a happy home, and to the gang with whom I get to share great food with on a regular basis.

To Emma, Lucy and Josh for the privilege of cooking for such an appreciative audience. Thank you to my editor David Joy for putting up with my pedantry and steering me on the right course. And last but never least my wonderful husband for photographing – and eating – tons of puddings to make this book. Not only are you a brilliant photographer you are my rock, thank you. **Elaine**.

The publishers acknowledge with thanks the support of Welcome to Yorkshire and Yorkshire Post Newspapers.

Welcome to Yorkshire
yorkshire.com

CONTENTS

Foreword

by Rosemary Shrager

'This is a book I have been waiting for.'

The Great Book of Yorkshire Pudding warms the cockles of my heart. It brings back childhood memories of my mother cooking her big square pudding under the dripping roast beef which she would cut into large pieces – I always had the biggest.

It also reminds me what real food is all about.

I feel very strongly we need to go back to the basics of cooking and re-establishing the lost techniques that seem to be drifting away through the pace of life, smart technology or just sheer laziness. Yorkshire puddings are one such thing. They are so quick and easy to make once understood, in fact by the end of this book you won't have to think about it, you'll just do it!

Elaine Lemm is the perfect person to write a book on Yorkshire pudding, with her solid Yorkshire roots, amazing knowledge of food and her pure sense of fun and enthusiasm.

Cooking should be fun and cooking and eating Yorkshire pudding is definitely the fun part.

Rosemary Shrager

Introduction

For as long as I can remember one of my father's favourite expressions was "never marry a woman who can't make Yorkshire puddings." As a child I never really understood what he meant as my earliest food memory is my grandmother lifting a tray of risen, golden puddings from her Yorkshire Range and eating my mother's perfect puddings every Sunday of my childhood. It never crossed my mind that anyone couldn't make them.

Sunday lunch with Yorkshire puddings was an intrinsic part of my growing up and even today the scent of a roast in the oven and the puddings cooking transports me back to our kitchen with Family Favourites on the radio and Mum singing along to Johnny Mathis as we prepared the lunch.

Over the years I have cooked Yorkshires around the globe, from Australia to the US, in Mexico and every Sunday when I lived in France (much to the amusement of the French who have never quite understood the quaint British habit but enjoyed them anyway) and I have yet to meet someone who doesn't like them. But what is it about the humble mixture of milk, eggs, flour and salt that has kept this dish a major part of British life with a worldwide interest for over four centuries?

When I began research for this book I thought I would find a clear and definitive answer but alas I have to say that no, I didn't. What I did find is mention Yorkshire puddings and a lively, and sometimes heated, conversation is guaranteed. Everyone it seems has an opinion about the origins, the folklore, the making, cooking and serving of the puds. As a member of the Guild of Food Writers I asked fellow members for their opinions and thus began one of the longest forum postings I have ever seen. I even received an e-mail from a Navajo Indian in Arizona who discovered the pudding recipe on my website and now makes them every week.

I still cook Yorkshires practically every Sunday and love watching my family devour them by the dozen – including their favourite of leftover puds dipped in toffee sauce –and my husband assures me that my father's sentiments on a wife being able to cook them is absolutely right.

Elaine Lemm *August 2010*

IN PRAISE OF YORKSHIRE PUDDINGS

Light brown moon in a gravy sky
Round O of delight on a big white plate
Floppy as a vest if you get 'em out early;
Hard as a wall if you get 'em out late!

Alchemy of eggs and milk and flour
Aesthetically gorgeous in a kitchenful of steam
Cultural symbol with enduring power;
Perfect as a sunset, elusive as a dream.

All in the wrist to get the air in the batter
As the shattered eggshells lie crushed like martyrs
As they wait to grace your Sunday platter:
The Yorkshire Pudding is the Queen of Starters!

My blood is racing and my heart is thudding
At the thought of this dinnertime's Yorkshire Pudding!

Ian McMillan

Yorkshire pudding spans the generations and the world. Amelie Taphouse from Perth, Western Australia, is clearly in seventh heaven.

Part 1

The History of the Yorkshire Pudding

The origin of the Yorkshire pudding is, as yet, unknown. There are no cave drawings, hieroglyphics and so far, no one has unearthed a Roman Yorkshire pudding dish buried beneath the streets of York. The puddings may have been brought to these shores by any of the invading armies across the centuries but unfortunately any evidence of this has yet to be discovered.

So it is to 1737 we have to go for the earliest, so far, printed reference for a 'dripping pudding'. The reference appears in an anonymous compendium of recipes called *The Whole Duty of a Woman*:

> *'Make a good batter as for pancakes; put in a hot toss-pan over the fire with a bit of butter to fry the bottom a little then put the pan and butter under a shoulder of mutton, instead of a dripping pan, keeping frequently shaking it by the handle and it will be light and savoury, and fit to take up when your mutton is enough; then turn it in a dish and serve it hot.'*

And similarly, John Bramley, a weaver living at Bramley near Leeds, recorded this scene;

> *Ther't meyt hung dahn afore t'fire to rooast,*
>
> *There's 't puddin'on t'brandree afore it ta tooast,*
>
> *Potatoes top o't'hob, they'll de don enif sooin,*
>
> *But Ah think tha can weive a few more bobbins bi nooin.*

From Peter Brears' Traditional Food in Yorkshire

The pancake batter was nothing new and had been used for centuries fried, cooked as fritters or boiled in oven cloths, but it was the placing of the batter under the roasting meat that transformed it into something that resembles what we now know as a Yorkshire pudding. Though the dripping pudding was thicker and flatter than a modern pudding it was also much richer in flavour because of the drippings and the fat from the meat. The meat mentioned is a shoulder of mutton but any meat could be used.

Skip forward another ten years and the word Yorkshire appears alongside the pudding in Hannah Glasse's recipe in *The Art of Cookery Made Easy*. Hannah is not a Yorkshire woman, but the illegitimate daughter of a prosperous gentleman, and was brought up with his family in Hexham, Northumberland. Why her recipe credits the pudding to Yorkshire is unknown, and rumours that a Yorkshire recipe was in existence at this time has yet to be proven.

Glasse's description 'take a stew-pan and put some dripping in, set it on the fire, when it boils, pour in your pudding' was used by food historian Jennifer Stead in her renowned essay, Yorkshire Pudding and Parkin', when she charmingly links the dish to the Yorkshire character:

'The fact that they require spanking hot fat, explosions as the batter hits it, fierce heat and crisp result, may explain why it has often been said that only Yorkshire folk – those possessing the Yorkshire temperament can make a true Yorkshire pudding.'

Yorkshire Pudding – the Nation's Favourite Regional Food

Yorkshire pudding is a regional food but with a nationwide appeal. In a poll, it beat Cornish pasties and the Melton Mowbray pie as the nation's favourite food.

A Yorkshire Pudding

Hannah Glasse 1747

Take a quart of milk, four eggs, and a little salt, make it up into a thick batter with flour, like a pancake batter. You must have a good piece of meat at the fire, take a stew-pan and put some dripping in, set it on the fire, when it boils, pour in your pudding, let it bake on the fire till you think it is high enough, then turn a plate upside-down in the dripping-pan, that the dripping may not be blacked; set your stew-pan on it under your meat, and let the dripping drop on the pudding, and the heat of the fire come to it, to make it of a fine brown. When your meat is done and set to table, drain all the fat from your pudding, and set it on the fire again to dry a little; then slide it as dry as you can into a dish, melt some butter, and pour into a cup, and set in the middle of the pudding. It is an exceeding good pudding, the gravy of the meat eats well with it.

More than a century later the Yorkshire pudding made its appearance in the weighty tome, *Mrs. Beeton's Book of Household Management*. Mrs. Beeton may have been one of Britain's most famous food writers but, unlike Hannah Glasse, her Yorkshire pudding recipe omitted one of the fundamental rules for making pudding – the need for the hottest oven possible. The recipe was further wrong by stating to cook the pudding in advance before placing it under the meat an hour before needed. Yorkshire folk blamed her error on her southern origins.

Yorkshire Pudding Day is the first Sunday in February

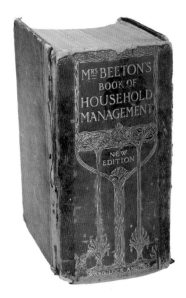

Yorkshire pudding featured in 1866 in the weighty tome *Mrs Beeton's Book of Household Management,* although the recipe was seriously flawed.

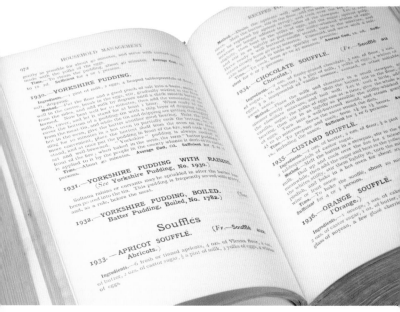

Mrs Beeton's Recipe – 1866

    1½ pints milk
    6 large tbsp flour
    3 eggs
    1 saltspoon salt

Put the flour into a basin with the salt and gradually stir in enough milk to make it a stiff batter.

When it is perfectly smooth and all the lumps are well rubbed down, add the remaining milk and the eggs, which should be well beaten.

Beat the mixture for a few minutes.

Pour into a shallow baking tin, which has been previously well rubbed with beef dripping.

Put the pudding into the oven.

Bake it for an hour.

Then, for another 30 minutes, place it under the meat, to catch a little of the gravy that flows from it.

Cut the pudding into small square pieces, put them on a hot dish and serve.

If the meat is baked, the pudding may at once be placed under it, resting the former on a small three cornered stand.

Time: 1½ hour.

Sufficient for 5 or 6 persons.

Seasonable at any time.

The Yorkshire pudding had made its way not only onto the plates of the nation but across the world. By the middle of the nineteenth century, the British Empire was the largest and richest empire in the world and as the British headed out to the colonies and pioneers to the new worlds of Australia, New Zealand and the Americas they took the Yorkshire pudding recipe with them.

The following, familiar looking recipe appears in the American book, *Practical Cooking and Dinner Giving*, by Mary Newton Foote Henderson in 1877.

Breakfast Puffs, or Pop-overs (Mrs Hopkins).

Ingredients:

Two cupfuls of milk,
two cupfuls of flour,
two eggs
an even tea-spoonful of salt.

Beat the eggs separately and well, add the whites last and then beat all well together. They may be baked in roll-pans, or deep gen-pans, which should be heated on the range and greased before the batter is put in : they should be filled half full with the batter. Or they may be baked in tea-cups, of which eight would be required for this quantity of batter. When baked serve immediately. For Graham gems use half Graham flour.

In the USA Yorkshire puddings are still known as Popovers today.

As Britain marched into the 20th century, it took the Yorkshire pudding with it. In an article in the Guardian in June 1940 discussing the merits of communal cooking, a reader known only as C.S recalls an East Anglian childhood, when the Boer was the conflict then engaging the elders but to them it remained an adult affair:

"On Sundays just before we all set out for the morning service, they recall, one of us would be sent to Mrs C's, along the street with the Sunday dinner. The Yorkshire pudding would flop around in the tin, and the joint of beef, resting on a wire grid which stood in the batter, was apt to slide about, so we had to go carefully. It seems to me now, they continue, that the pudding should have been overcooked long before the meat was done, but the dinner was always perfect when it was brought back, piping hot by one of the boys."

During two world wars, the Yorkshire pudding kept bellies full when meat was in short supply. They were even made quite successfully using dried egg when the ration of 1 egg per week was introduced in 1941. And, it was around this time the famous British comedian Stanley Holloway recorded his delightful monologue on Yorkshire Pudden written by Weston and Lee.

I love Yorkshire pudding but I was nearly turned off it at prep school because one day a week they used to serve it with treacle, which I hated. I would do anything to avoid going to school on Tuesdays!

Dame Judi Dench

In the 19th century beef was often cooked by hanging it from a bottle-jack. This one is in York Castle Museum. Photo © York Castle Museum

The Yorkshire pudding survived the wars, the food rationing of the forties and fifties, and sailed through the swinging sixties. However, as the pace of modern life picked up and more women worked, cooking in the home started to fall. The rise of convenience foods and ready meals towards the end of the last century saw the invention of the first commercially produced Yorkshire puddings with the launch of the Yorkshire based Aunt Bessie's brand in 1995.

In 2007, Vale of York MP Anne McIntosh campaigned for Yorkshire puddings to be given the same protected status as French champagne or Greek feta cheese,

"The people of Yorkshire are rightly and fiercely proud of the Yorkshire pudding," she said. "It is something which has been cherished and perfected for centuries in Yorkshire."

At the time Yorkshire pudding was deemed too generic a term but that hasn't stopped Aunt Bessie's and two other pudding manufacturers with support of the Regional Food Group for Yorkshire and Humber making another attempt for the protected status. Understandably, this has caused concern from everyone outside of Yorkshire who makes the puddings commercially. Roast Beef and Yorkshire-Style puddings?

Today the Yorkshire pudding is as popular as ever whether home-cooked, eaten at the thousands of restaurants across the UK serving a traditional Sunday lunch, or bought in from the supermarket. On a Sunday ex-pat Brits throughout Europe and the rest of the world tuck into Yorkshire pudding and in Australia, New Zealand and Canada puddings are still a large part of the food culture. Just why this simple mixture of flour, eggs, milk and salt gained a place in the culinary hearts of a nation, and a worldwide reputation, is a mystery which many have tried to solve but have yet to find the answer. Maybe it is simply because they taste so good?

Stanley Holloway Monologue

Written by R.P. Weston and Bert Lee (1940)

Yorkshire Pudden!

Hi waitress, excuse me a minute, now listen,
I'm not finding fault, but here, Miss,
The 'taters look gradely… the beef is a'reet,
But what kind of pudden is this?

It's what?…
Yorkshire pudden!, now coom, coom, coom, coom,
It's what? Yorkshire pudden d'ye say!
It's pudden, I'll grant you… it's some sort of pudden,
But not Yorkshire pudden… nay nay!

The real Yorkshire pudden's a dream in batter,
To make one's an art, not a trade,
Now listen to me, for I'm going to tell thee,
How t' first Yorkshire pudden wor made.

A young angel on furlough from heaven,
Came flying above Ilkley Moor,
And this angel, poor thing, got cramp in her wing,
And coom down at owd woman's door.

The owd woman smiled and said, 'Ee, it's an angel,
Well I am surprised to see thee,
I've not seen an angel before… but thou 'rt welcome,
I'll make thee a nice cup o' tea.'

The angel said, 'Ee, thank you kindly, I will',
Well, she had two or three cups of tea,
Three or four Sally Lunns, and a couple of buns…
Angels eat very lightly you see.

The owd woman looking at clock said, 'By Gum!
He's due home from mill is my Dan,
You get on wi' ye tea, but you must excuse me,
I must make pudden now for t' owd man.

Then the angel jumped up and said, 'Gimme the bowl…
Flour and watter and eggs, salt an' all,
And I'll show thee how we make puddens in Heaven,
For Peter and Thomas and Paul'.

So t' owd woman gave her the things, and the angel,
Just pushed back her wings and said. 'Hush'
Then she tenderly tickled the mixture wi' t' spoon,
Like an artist would paint with his brush.

Aye, she mixed up that pudden with Heavenly magic,
She played with her spoon on that dough,
Just like Paderewski would play the piano.
Or Kreisler now deceased would twiddle his bow.

And then it wor done and she put it in t' oven
She said t' owd woman, 'Goodbye',
Then she flew away leaving the first Yorkshire pudden,
That ever was made… and that's why…

It melts in the mouth, like the snow in the sunshine,
As light as a maiden's first kiss,
As soft as the fluff on the breast of a dove…
Not elephant's leather, like this.

It's real Yorkshire pudden that makes Yorkshire lassies,
So buxum and broad in the hips,
It's real Yorkshire pudden that makes Yorkshire cricketers,
Win County championships.

It's real Yorkshire pudden that gives me my dreams,
Of a real Paradise up above,
Where at the last trump, I'll queue up for a lump,
Of the real Yorkshire pudden I love.

And there on a cloud… far away from the crowd,
In a real Paradise, not a dud 'un,
I'll do nowt for ever… and ever and ever,
But gollup up real Yorkshire pudden.

Why is a Yorkshire Pudding Called a Pudding when it is not a Pudding?

The confusion that Yorkshire pudding is not a sweet pudding lies in the understanding that until the mid 17th century the majority of British puddings were savoury. These puddings were similar to sausages with meat forced into a skin then boiled or fried. Or they were puddings boiled in pudding cloths – think steak and kidney pudding.

By the second half of the 18th century traditional English puddings no longer included meat and by the 19th, though puddings were still boiled, they more resembled cakes. The survivors of the earliest puddings seen in the modern kitchen are black pudding, white pudding and, of course, the haggis.

Interestingly, the British plum pudding, now so loved at Christmas, was also once a savoury dish – a mixture of beef and mutton, dried fruit and flavoured with wine and spices – and was the accompaniment to beef long before Yorkshire took over.

The World's Largest Yorkshire Pudding

In 1996, members of the Skipton Round Table made the largest-ever Yorkshire pudding at Broughton Hall, just outside the town. According to Guinness World Records, the pudding measured an astounding 500 sq ft.

Yorkshire Frugality or Skill?

"Them as has most pudding can have most meat."
A favourite Yorkshire saying.

In Yorkshire, the puddings were traditionally served as a starter for Sunday lunch and unjust allegations cite frugality and the meanness of Yorkshire folk as the reason – the filling puddings meant less meat would be eaten. In defence of my fellow Yorkshiremen, the accusers would do well to consider the following.

Today it is possible to walk into any supermarket, butcher's shop or farmers' market and the choice of affordable meat is overwhelming, but this has not always been the case. Meat is relatively less expensive today than in the past and, even as recently as the 1960s, for many the luxury of a lavish joint of meat on a Sunday was impossible. So the joint would be small and as families generally were larger in number, this meant the meat had a long way to go. So the pudding helped eke out the meat.

Work for many was more manual than we are used to in the technology assisted world of today and the filling-quality of the Yorkshire pudding was essential to keep bellies full.

In the last century there were long periods when meat was scarce. Although food rationing wasn't introduced until the latter end of the First World War, in the Second World War it began early on. Fresh eggs too were rationed, but powdered eggs produced a reasonable Yorkshire pudding - though I am told they never rose quite the same. With Yorkshire puddings as a starter, the canny housewife could provide a substantial, satisfying and economical family lunch throughout these adversities.

The mighty Yorkshire pudding, therefore, though deemed a poor man's fare actually made a virtue out of a necessity, not out of frugality and certainly not meanness.

What is the Perfect Yorkshire Pudding?

A Yorkshire pudding is Carbohydrate + H_2O + protein + NaCl + lipids, not an enticing description but this is what it is according to the Royal Society of Chemistry – in chemical terms at least.

In 2008 the society was approached by an Englishman living in the Rockies in the USA seeking scientific advice on the chemistry of the dish following a string of kitchen flops. Ian Lyness had contacted the RSC to get an explanation for why his attempts at cooking traditional Yorkshire puddings in Colorado had gone flat despite success in other parts of the country. The RSC is now checking with fellow scientists to see if cooking the famed dish in a mountain climate would lead to pressure problems.

The society, which has thousands of members working in the foods and drinks industries, including top chef Heston Blumenthal, used the query to ascertain the correct way to prepare a Yorkshire pudding.

Calls to, and from, various parts of the UK led the Royal Society of Chemistry to conclude that for a Yorkshire pudding to be judged successful it had to be no less than 10cm / 4" in height.

Chemical scientist and author John Emsley, of Yorkshire, also daringly claimed that people not from that county rarely produced worthy Yorkshire puddings. The RSC invited Dr Emsley to define Yorkshire pudding, by delving into the lore of his home county to produce the definitive recipe.

"It is wonderful as a starter and main course, as we all know," he said. "However, we have lost sight of it as a superb dessert to follow the main meal and we should aspire to bring it back again as a genuine pudding after many years absence."

The Royal Society of Chemistry
Perfect Yorkshire Pudding

Ingredients

Tablespoon and a half of plain flour
1 egg
Half milk, half water to make a thin batter
Half a teaspoon of salt.

Method

Put flour in a bowl, make a well in the middle, add the egg, stir until the two are combined then start gradually adding the milk and water combining as you go.

Add the liquid until the batter is a smooth and thin consistency.

Stir in half teaspoon of salt and leave to stand for 10 minutes

Put beef dripping into Yorkshire pudding tins or into one large tin but don't use too much fat.

Put into hot oven until the fat starts to smoke.

Give the batter a final stir and pour into the tin or tins.

Place in hot oven until well risen - should take 10 to 15 minutes.

Serve

Always serve as a separate course before the main meal and use the best gravy made from the juices of the roast joint. Yorkshire housewives served Yorkshire pudding before the meal so that they would eat less of the more expensive main course.

NB: When the batter is made it must not be placed in the fridge but be kept at room temperature.

A perfect meal with perfect Yorkshire puddings.

Part 2 – Cooking

Perfect Yorkshire Puddings – Every Time

There is no definitive recipe for making Yorkshire puddings – everyone it seems has their own and this is mine. It isn't the method my mother showed me as she has the knack of making amazing puddings without measuring anything, but is one I have developed over the years to produce perfect puddings every time:

Serves 6

4 large, fresh eggs, measured in a jug
Equal quantity of milk to eggs
Equal quantity of plain flour to eggs
Pinch of salt
Lard, beef dripping or vegetable oil for cooking

Heat the oven to the highest temperature possible. However, do not exceed 230°C/450 °F/Gas 8 or the fat may burn.

Pour the eggs and milk into a large mixing bowl and add the pinch of salt. Whisk thoroughly with an electric or hand whisk until foamy. Leave to stand for about 10 minutes to allow the bubbles to subside.

Sieve the flour into the milk and egg mixture and beat again using an electric or hand-whisk to create a lump free batter resembling thick cream. Finally pass the batter through a sieve into another bowl or jug.

Leave the batter to rest in the kitchen for a minimum of 30 minutes up to a couple of hours, the longer the better.

Place a pea-sized piece of lard, dripping or ½ tsp vegetable oil in a Yorkshire pudding tin (4 x 5cm/2" hole tin) or 12-hole muffin tin and heat in the oven until the fat is smoking.

Give the batter another good whisk adding 2 tbsp of cold water and fill a third of each section of the tin with batter and return quickly to the oven.

Leave to cook until risen and golden brown, approx 20 minutes. Repeat the last step again without adding any water until all the batter is used up.

Step by Step Yorkshire Pudding Recipe

Serves 6

Equipment needed:

Measuring jug
Mixing bowl
Whisk – electric or hand
Fine sieve
4-hole Yorkshire pudding tin or a 12-hole muffin tin

Ingredients

4 large, fresh eggs, measured in a jug
Equal quantity of milk to eggs
Equal quantity of plain flour to eggs
Pinch of salt
Lard, beef dripping or vegetable oil for cooking

In Advance:

Heat the oven to the highest temperature possible. However, do not exceed 230°C/450 °F/Gas 8 or the fat may burn.

Step 1

Pour the eggs and milk into a large mixing bowl and add the pinch of salt. Whisk thoroughly with an electric or hand whisk until foamy. Leave to stand for about 10 minutes to allow the bubbles to subside.

Step 2

Sieve the flour into the egg, milk and salt mixture. Beat again using an electric or hand-whisk to create a lump free batter resembling thick cream. Finally pass the batter through a sieve into another bowl or jug. Leave the batter to rest in the kitchen for a minimum of 30 minutes up to a couple of hours - the longer the better.

Step 3

Place a pea-sized piece of lard, dripping or ½ tsp vegetable oil into the Yorkshire pudding or muffin tin and heat in the oven until the fat is smoking.

Step 4

Give the batter another good whisk adding 2 tbsp of cold water. Fill a third of each section of the tin with batter and return quickly to the oven.

Step 5

Leave to cook until risen and golden brown, approx 20 minutes. Repeat the last step again without adding any water until all the batter is used up.

Step 6

Serve either as a starter dish with hot gravy, or as part of a Sunday roast.

Choosing a Yorkshire Pudding Tin

You have the perfect recipe and have gathered together the ingredients. Next is what tin (or pan if you are outside the UK) to use?

Choosing a Yorkshire pudding tin is easy – it depends simply on what size of pudding you want to make. A Yorkshire pudding can be made in any dish, tray or pan as long as it can withstand the high temperature required for cooking. I have never had great success with glass, even Pyrex, but some swear by them. When stuck, I have used a copper frying pan, a Swiss roll tin and Victoria sponge tins.

The most commonly used tin is a 4-cup tin, known as a muffin top pan in the USA. The 4-cup makes sideplate-sized Yorkshire puddings which are perfect as a starter or served with the meat.

For the traditional large rectangular pudding, or a big Toad in the Hole, you will need, surprise, surprise, a large rectangular roasting tin. The tin needs to be heavy and preferably with a thick bottom enabling it to reach a high temperature comfortably. Perfect for a smaller Toad in the Hole or square pudding is a 20 cm x 8" roasting tin.

A 12-hole muffin tin makes a good-sized pudding for individual puddings to serve with the meat and vegetables.

For canapé sized puddings, a 24-hole mini muffin tin works best.

Yorkshire pudding tins supplied by Lakeland, with 48 stores across the UK or check online at http://www.lakeland.co.uk

My Yorkshire Puddings Won't Rise!

A tray of Yorkshire puddings fresh from the oven should be well-risen, golden brown with a crisp exterior and soft middle but like everything sometimes they fail. There may be several reasons why, so here's a few tips to help solve the problem.

- Use equal volumes of egg, milk and flour. Too much flour and the resulting puddings will be heavy and stodgy. Without enough egg, there will be insufficient air beaten in for a successful rise.

- The batter must be lump free.

- Leave the batter to rest for a minimum of 30 minutes up to several hours in a cool place – not the refrigerator. Resting the batter softens the starch grains and causes them to swell. Resting also allows the gluten to relax resulting in light, fluffy puddings.

- Avoid overfilling the tin, a third is usually sufficient. Too much batter and the puddings will begin to rise but soon collapse as they will be too heavy.

- A successful rise comes from a cold batter, into hot fat and quickly into a very hot oven. To make sure the batter is cool, add 2 tbsp of cold water before pouring into the lightly smoking hot fat.

- If possible, avoid using a fan oven as the forced air, if too strong, can cause the puddings to collapse.

- Never use olive oil or butter to cook the puddings as they cannot reach a high enough temperature without burning.

- Avoid opening the door during cooking, the cold air will make the puddings collapse. They may recover but never rise as high as before.

- Do not wash Yorkshire pudding tins as this spoils the surface of the tins and can prevent puddings from rising. Simply wipe clean with kitchen paper after use.

Yorkshire Pudding Calculator

Ever wondered how much Yorkshire pudding batter to make, then this handy little calculator should help. The batter is made using my recipe of equal quantities of flour to egg and milk. The best batter is made with a minimum of 2 eggs.

	12 or 6 hole muffin tin	4-hole tin	30 x 24 cm 12 x 9 ½" tin	18 x 23cm 7 x 9" tin
2 egg mix	12	8	1	2
4 egg mix	24	16	2	4
6 egg mix	36	24	3	6

My grandmother made the best Yorkshires ever – they were cooked in a big round tin with hot lard in a coal oven and rose at least six inches. They were light and fluffy and crispy on the outside and my grandfather always said the trick was that they had been kissed by an angel. We had them for starters with onion gravy, alongside the meat and sometimes for pudding with lemon juice and sugar (I'd have had all three if allowed). I have done everything she taught me – lots of beating, leave to stand, make sure the fat is piping hot, don't open the oven door until the time is up, don't slam the kitchen door whilst they're in the oven – and never achieved what she did. Mine are rather flat, pathetic little things. Shame!

Jenni Murray (BBC Radio 4 Woman's Hour Presenter and Journalist)

Myths or Useful Tips?

Ask how do you make your Yorkshire puddings and be prepared for the onslaught of answers. It seems everyone has their own recipe and secret 'tips' for the perfect pud with some, apparently, handed down from generation to generation.

The myths relating to the ideal pudding may at first glance seem a little whacky, but when looked at a little deeper they are not always so silly. Certain suggestions are in direct contradiction and others a touch xenophobic. Here are a few of my favourites:

- Always mix the pudding outside in the fresh air. This is not so strange as I first thought. Today we have extractor fans but try mixing Yorkshire puddings in a hot, steamy kitchen with a roaring fire in the background.

- Dinner lady Margaret Hullah, on retiring after feeding fresh-faced pilots across Yorkshire air bases for 29 years, finally divulged her secret for perfect puddings – keep all doors and windows closed.

- Use the first fresh fall of snow to create a cold batter.

- Yorkshire puddings made outside the county never rise.

- Yorkshire puddings taste best when mixed by a Yorkshire hand.

- Mix puddings standing up – mix puddings sitting down. A fork is best (my mother) – only use a spoon. Always add – never add ...

- If the Yorkshires fail to rise there's trouble in't bedroom?

- If the Yorkshire puddings go wrong it is always the oven's fault.

Suffice to say, if it works for you, great!

The Great Yorkshire Pudding Contest

The contest held in Leeds saw five native chefs humiliated by Mr Tin Sung Chan who took the top prize. The taste of the pudding according to the judges was superb and it was reported that the pudding rose to the height of a coronation crown.

Asked the secret of his success, Chan, chef at the Chopsticks Restaurant, said, "I put in a secret ingredient. It's a Chinese herb called tai luk." Tai luk, as it turned out, does not exist! It was Mr Chan's private joke, as is the precise cooking time in the recipe.

Tin Sung Chan Recipe for Yorkshire Pudding

1/2 pt milk
4 eggs
Just under 1/2 tsp salt
Dash of pepper
1/2 tsp tai luk
1/2 lb plain flour, sifted
Pre-heat the oven to mark 8, 450 deg. F.

Mix all the ingredients except the flour, beating well together (I used the food processor). Let stand for 15 minutes, then beat in the flour. Heat dripping or oil in a roasting tin in the oven until smoking hot, then pour in the batter and cook for 20 minutes 52.2 seconds.

Mit Custard!

by Stephanie Moon

My favourite memory of Yorkshire pudding is of a time in Germany as a young commis chef working at the Four Seasons hotel on Maximillian Strasse in Munich.

On a day off a group of my chef friends decided to cook their home dishes for the others to try and I was making the classic roast beef and Yorkshire pudding. They all watched on in amazement as the Yorkies rose to the occasion and did me proud. The rib of roast beef was ruddy and rare, and the pan juices made a good gravy, but the Yorkshire pudding was the jewel in the crown in all its glory.

I placed the pudding with the beef on the table and one German chef's eyes popped open, and he exclaimed, "But I thought you EEngleesh always served pudding mit custard!"

Many people know Yorkshire puddings the world over. Having worked in Germany, Switzerland, America and Australia, chefs and locals alike say when you tell them where you are from: "Oh home of the Yorkshire pudding."

Having eaten some Yorkies the consistency of washleathers and others that are as dry as volcanic ash, I guess everyone has a different take on the Yorkie but the recipe I use has been the same for the last 22 years of my culinary career and has not let me down yet.

Stephanie Moon's Recipe

Here is my secret...

Simply equal quantities of eggs (ideally free range to give a brighter colour and the feel good factor), whole milk – no semi-skimmed here folks – and plain good flour. Being a Yorkshire cook I buy all three ingredients locally but if you can buy local-to-you

Stephanie Moon in Clocktower Kitchen.

rather than mass produced products it will taste better for sure.

Just mix the three ingredients together – lumps are not an option! Then add a big pinch of salt and sieve into a clean jug.

Heat the Yorkshire pudding moulds in the oven half full of fat or oil.

Before you pour your batter in, just check there is no Cappuccino-style foam on the top of the mixture. Remove this if there is before pouring in the batter.

Try to pour directly into the centre of each mould. This avoids the batter from splitting open in the well of the mould and your Yorkie being split at the top when it is cooked.

Hot oven to begin 180°C, then seven minutes later turn this down to 160°C for another few mins.

May all your Yorkshire Puddings be crowning garlands of joy!

The Yorkshire Pudding Express

by Rob Green, Green's Restaurant, Whitby

Ok, so I'm on a train, it's Yorkshire Day and I've got a three-course meal to cook and serve for twenty of North Yorkshire's finest dignitaries. The kitchen is the size of a buffet trolley and the oven is rubbish, as expected.

My guests will dismiss all of the above and expect the finest cuisine known to man.

The menu – a trio of Whitby lobster, roasted Yorkshire fillet of beef, with of course those copper coloured puddings from Yorkshire, a curd tart for dessert and cheese to finish – seemed like a good idea at the time. Most of the preparation has been done at Green's Restaurant beforehand. The lobster bisque, lobster mousse and the Yorkshire curd tarts sit proudly on a narrow shelf in the train's 'kitchen'.

Some things have to be cooked real time. This includes the roast fillet, the red wine gravy and, most importantly, the Yorkshire puddings.

The carriages are hitched up with an almighty clank, pushing the kitchen train about two feet down the track and spilling half my lobster bisque all over the place. From now on everything is placed on the floor and me and my son Ben – who is assisting me in the kitchen – now have to stand like boxers waiting for the next blow to strike. The guests arrive and we set off in a haze of steam.

The timing for this event is crucial. Two of the four courses have to be served before we arrive at our destination and the other two on the return journey. The Yorkshire puddings are put into the oven before we start to plate up the starters.

The oven is no good. The fillet of roasted beef is not yet cooked and it needs time to rest. Everything stops now and all my energy

Twenty-four of the finest Yorkshire puddings made by Rob Green and his son Ben on the 'Pickering Express'.

is directed at the puddings. The prime fillet of Yorkshire beef is relegated to the grill above the oven to finish cooking and resting, while the gravy slops around in a pan on the stove, as the steam train pulls us closer to our destination.

The oven door is closed once more and I start praying, swearing, and plating up the starters.

The puddings have now become an obsession. If they're not ready in fifteen minutes it's certain 'Death on the Pickering Express' for Mr Green. The empty plates from the starters come back, and I peak inside the dark abyss of the oven.........

YES ! There they are. Twenty-four of the finest Yorkshire infantry standing to attention, primed and ready for battle. An immense feeling of calm comes over me. I would never live it down serving rubbish Yorkshire puddings on Yorkshire Day to Yorkshire's finest.

The rest of the day goes splendidly; all the guests are happy and completely unaware of my ' highway to hell' train journey.

If your vegetables are a little underdone and your meat a little overdone, don't worry. Just make sure those puddings are tip top and peace on earth will prevail. Well, in Yorkshire at least.

Rob Green

Recipes

Starters, Mains, Dessert, Leftovers and Parties

Yorkshire puddings are most often thought of as the starter or appearing on the main course of a traditional Sunday lunch. Though they are best recognised in this role they can and do materialise in many other guises. They materialise as starters, have become main courses in their own right, and make delicious desserts. Leftovers are never thrown away – certainly not in Yorkshire – and miniature puds even make great party guests.

Yorkshire Pudding as a Starter

When served as a starter, Yorkshire pudding is traditionally served with gravy made from the dark, caramelised drippings of the meat, or a thick onion gravy. But, there is currently a revival for some of the forgotten ways to serve the puddings. One custom was to drizzle the pudding with raspberry vinegar as a starter, though renowned food writer Maxine Clark remembers her Yorkshire-born grandfather eating his puddings and raspberry vinegar for dessert (see recipe page 76). If you don't have time to make your own vinegar, Yorkshire-based Womersley Foods produce a sweet, syrupy vinegar, perfect for puddings. I was initially sceptical about this combination but having tried it, it is delicious.

Yorkshire pudding with raspberry vinegar – delicious!

Other vinegary concoctions include a sprinkle of malt vinegar, mint sauce and my mother made what she calls a Yorkshire "Sauerkraut", also known as a Yorkshire Ploughman's Salad. Finely shredded lettuce and sliced onions are soaked in malt vinegar and sweetened with just enough sugar to give a sweet-sour taste – the only way to judge the right balance is by dipping a finger in and tasting. In summer thin slices of Dad's home grown cucumbers, or fresh mint, would also be added to the mixture. The 'salad' makes a great condiment for cold meats, cheeses or pork pie but really comes into its own on a hot, golden Yorkshire pudding.

All the starter dishes above use a plain batter but food historian Peter Brears in his book *Traditional Food in Yorkshire* has a lovely list of flavoured batters:

115g/4 oz of minced meat sprinkled over the batter just after pouring into the tin.

Thinly sliced onion in the bottom of the tin.

A large boiled onion, finely chopped and mixed into the batter with a teaspoon of sage – to serve with pork or mutton.

115g/4 oz finely grated Cheshire cheese mixed into the batter.

55g/2oz currants mixed into the batter, again to serve with pork.

Yorkshire Pudding as a Main Course

In these more comfortable times, and filling up with puddings as a starter no longer imperative, the pudding now jostles for space on the plate with the meat and the veg. It has become a support rather than the main act on the Sunday lunch stage with resentment in Yorkshire that the 'southerner's' habit (serving puds with the main course) as they call it has usurped tradition.

The demise is more than made up for with the expansion of the repertoire of the Yorkshire pudding; they are no longer simply a Sunday treat providing instead the perfect padding for midweek lunches and suppers.

Filled Yorkshire puddings are extremely popular both in the home and in dining pubs throughout the UK. The large pudding with its risen sides serves as the perfect receptacle for meats, stews, veggies, cauliflower cheese, chilli, baked beans, in fact, anything that requires serving in a bowl. Recipes for filled Yorkshire puddings can be found on page 51.

I remember as a fresh-faced student at Scarborough Technical College, being invited to cook for the Jurade de St. Emilion, one of the wealthiest, most respected wine councils in the world. This was through College and the feast was to be Yorkshire Fayre – what else!! Then of course Roast Beef with Yorkshire Pudding was to be the main course. The whole proceedings were filmed for regional television as the owners of such Chateaux or Cheval Blanc, Monbousquet and other Grand Cru Greats tucked into our northern offering. The verdict "tres bien, c'est fameaux!" I think that they liked it and we celebrated as only a teenager can in South-West France with a glass or two of wine. Sante!

Andrew Pern, Chef-Owner the Star Inn at Harome, North Yorkshire

Yorkshire Pudding as a Pudding

That Yorkshire pudding is not a pudding makes it quite confusing to serve it as a pudding. One the UK's most famous food-writers the late Jane Grigson (mother of celebrity chef Sophie Grigson) tells a lovely story in her book, *English Food* (1977), about her father's love of leftovers served with condensed milk.

> *On roast-beef Sundays, my mother's father, who had reached heights of power and respectability in the Bank of England, forgot what was due to his position and remembered the ways of the Northumbrian farm at Old Bewick which his family had come from. The roast beef went back to the kitchen after the main course, but the Yorkshire pudding remained to be finished up with sweetened condensed milk. I do not know how my grandmother took this - she prided herself on her desserts - but my mother shared his delight in the crisp and sticky pudding. When she had a home of her own, and a family, she passed his taste on to us who only remembered him, in spats and spectacles and pin-striped trousers, from old photographs.*

Nutritionists today would no doubt be horrified by having Yorkshire puddings twice in the same meal, but surely flour, eggs and milk appear in many English puddings?

Large slices of apple, or chunks of rhubarb tossed into the batter after pouring into the tin make excellent desserts served with ice cream on top. Caramelised Apple Yorkshire pudding (page 74) pushes it to another level, and Sarah Beattie's match of Yorkshire pudding with chocolate is ingenious. (page 75).

Using Up the Leftover Yorkshire Pudding

Yorkshire folk are not easily given to throwing things away, least of all Yorkshire puddings, so have come up with means of serving the leftovers in many appealing ways.

Leftover Batter:

It is rare to have batter left over but sometimes there isn't quite enough to make another tray of puddings. But, as the batter is exactly the same as a pancake batter but thicker, it can be thinned down, covered and stored in the refrigerator to make pancakes the next day. The batter will turn a slightly grey colour. Don't worry just whisk, and it will brighten up again. Do not keep for more than one day.

The batter also freezes well, and though once defrosted isn't suitable for making Yorkshire puddings, can again be used for pancakes at a later date. For convenience, pour the thick batter into an ice cube tray and when frozen tip into a freezer bag. Fancy a pancake for breakfast? Defrost a cube or two, thin down, and away you go.

As the batter contains eggs and flour, leftover batter makes a good, easy and convenient, additive-free thickening for gravies, stews and soups. Freeze as above and one cube will nicely thicken a pint of liquid.

Yorkshire Pudding Ice Cream

Ice cream producers, Yummy Yorkshire, created the first Yorkshire Pudding Ice Cream, with Gravy and Raspberry Vinegar, for Yorkshire Day (August 1st). The gravy-flavoured creamy ice cream contained tiny lumps of Yorkshire pudding, an interesting salt-sweet flavour. You either love it or hate it!

Drizzling
Golden Syrup
onto
Yorkshire pudding.

Leftover Cooked Yorkshire Puddings:

Hard as it is to imagine, sometimes there are leftover Yorkshire puddings, which are far too delicious simply to throw away. Unfortunately, Yorkshire puddings don't reheat very well, turning dry and brittle in the process, though smothered in hot gravy they will soften a little.

The beauty of a Yorkshire pudding is it is happy with a sweet or savoury, hot or cold filling giving endless possibilities for the inventive cook. A friend's father liked two leftover Yorkshires with slices of beef in between as a sandwich at suppertime. A vegetarian friend recommends filling a pudding with cauliflower cheese and popping it under a grill for a few minutes to warm through.

For the sweet-toothed try them simply with milk and sugar or fancy with apple sauce and cinnamon. Pile up strawberries and whipped cream or cram the puddings with balls of different flavoured ice cream.

As a child, any puddings that weren't scoffed at Sunday lunch in our house reappeared on the table at tea time with a jar of jam, tin of Golden Syrup or treacle, which I still do today. I have even served leftover Yorkshire puddings with marmalade or lemon curd as a breakfast treat.

And, if the puddings have dried up and gone brittle, birds love them.

Party Puddings

Who would have thought that the Yorkshire pudding, once classed as poor man's food, is now an honoured guest at sophisticated parties, weddings, picnics and barbecues. Miniature Yorkshire puddings filled with rare beef and horseradish, sausages, onion gravy – in fact anything a normal pudding would hold – are the must-have canapé. The pudding makes a great holder for the inventive fillings and will hold its shape well making it the perfect finger food.

Filled Yorkshire Puddings

Yorkshire puddings are far too good to just accompany a Sunday roast. Large individual puddings filled with stews and gravies quickly become a meal in themselves for mid-week suppers or even as an alternative to the Sunday roast.

The risen sides of the pudding turn it into a bowl making simple, one dish serving. Great.

My grandfather loved to eat Yorkshire pudding with condensed milk as a pudding.

I'm with northerners on the large Yorkshire cooked in a big dish so that you get both crisp and crunchy and wonderfully soggy all in one. Surely that was the point of it anyway, to sit under the meat, catching the drips of cooking juices to make a first-rate filling preamble to the joint. Thrifty and delicious all in one.

I'm always immensely suspicious of individual Yorkshires – so often tough and chewy and over-cooked. In pubs and elsewhere I can't stop the words 'Aunt Bessie' wafting through my thoughts at the sight of them. Just plain wrong, unless you are, perhaps, going to have them for pud.

Celebrity chef and cookery writer Sophie Grigson

Chilli Filled Yorkshire Pudding

Serves 4

> 1 quantity of Yorkshire pudding batter (see page 26)
> 2 tbsp vegetable oil
> 1 large onion, peeled and roughly chopped
> 2 garlic cloves, peeled and roughly chopped
> 450g/1 lb lean, minced beef
> 2 tsp dried chopped chillies, or to taste
> 1 x 400g/14 oz can peeled, chopped tomatoes plus juice
> 1 x 400g/14 oz can red kidney beans, drained
> 1 tbsp Worcestershire sauce
> 1 tbsp tomato ketchup
> 1 tbsp chopped parsley
> Salt and Pepper
> Tabasco sauce (optional)

Make the Yorkshire pudding batter according to the recipe and leave to rest while making the chilli.

In a large roomy pan, heat the oil to medium hot, add the onion and cook until softened - about 5 minutes. Take care not to burn the onions. Add the garlic and cook for a further 2 minutes.

Raise the heat and add the minced beef. Stir continuously until all the meat is browned. Add the chillies and stir again.

Add the tomatoes and juice, followed by the drained red kidney beans. Stir again and cook for 5 minutes on a high heat, then add the Worcestershire sauce, tomato ketchup, lower the heat and cook for 45 minutes. Stir the sauce from time to time to prevent it sticking. If the sauce thickens too much the heat is too high, lower the heat and add a little boiling water to thin it out.

Heat the oven to the highest temperature possible, however, do not exceed 230°C/450°F/Gas 8 or the fat may burn.

Place a pea-sized piece of lard, dripping or ½tsp vegetable oil into 4 individual Yorkshire pudding, or 18cm Victoria sandwich tins

and heat in the oven until the fat is smoking.

Give the batter another good whisk adding 2 tbsp of cold water and fill a third of the tin with batter and return quickly to the oven. Cook for 20 - 25 minutes or until the pudding is golden and risen.

Once the chilli is cooked, add the parsley, stir, adjust the seasoning, and if you like more of a kick to the chilli add a few drops of Tabasco sauce (or put the sauce on the table so everyone can season to their preferred heat). Cook for a further 5 minutes.

Put the Yorkshire pudding on a dinner plate and fill with the cooked chilli.

Onion Gravy Filled Yorkshire Pudding

The simplest, quickest and delicious filling for giant Yorkshire puddings is an onion gravy. For a more substantial dish, add a few chunks of leftover roast meat, and vegetables from Sunday lunch. Smother with thick, glossy onion gravy – lovely.

Onion gravy is also perfect to serve with Toad in the Hole.

Serves 4

> 1 quantity of Yorkshire pudding batter (see page 26)
> 2 tbsp vegetable oil
> 2 tbsp butter
> 2 medium onions, peeled and thinly sliced
> ½ tsp sugar
> 1 tsp balsamic vinegar
> 750ml/ 1 ¼pt beef stock
> 4 tsp corn flour*
> 4 tsp cold water*
> Salt and black pepper

Make the Yorkshire pudding batter according to the recipe and leave to rest for a minimum of 30 minutes to several hours.

Heat the oven to the highest temperature possible, however, do not exceed 230°C/450°F/Gas 8 or the fat may burn.

Place a pea-sized piece of lard, dripping or ½tsp vegetable oil into 4 individual Yorkshire puddings, or 18cm Victoria sandwich tins and heat in the oven until the fat is smoking.

Give the batter another good whisk adding 2 tbsp of cold water and fill a third of the tin with batter and return quickly to the oven. Cook for 20 -25 minutes or until the pudding is golden and risen

Meanwhile, over a gentle heat, melt the oil and butter in a large saucepan. Add the onion and cover with a lid. Cook slowly for approx 10 minutes or until the onions are soft and translucent. Stir occasionally.

Add the sugar and balsamic vinegar to the onions and stir well. Cover with the lid and continue to cook for a further 5 minutes.

Add the stock and boil gently uncovered for 5 minutes.

In a heatproof jug or bowl mix the corn flour with the cold water to a thin paste*. Pour a little of the hot gravy into the starch mixture and mix thoroughly. Pour the starch mixture back into the gravy, raise the heat to high and boil for 10 minutes or until the gravy is slightly thickened. Keep warm until ready to serve over the Yorkshire puddings once cooked.

If you have leftover Yorkshire pudding batter use 2 tbsp to thicken the gravy. Pour a little of the hot gravy into the Yorkshire pudding batter, stir well then add back to the gravy, bring to the boil stirring constantly.

Any food writer on a newspaper gives a Yorkshire pudding recipe at their peril. Indignant readers from Lancashire tell you it's a Lancastrian dish, and everyone has the one and only authentic recipe, and it's not the one you just published. The great Clement Freud used to make his – can you believe it? – with self-raising flour – enough to make me very indignant indeed.

What I like in a good Yorkshire is the combination of the crisp risen bits and the hollow soggy bits – the hills and dales of Yorkshire. My grandmother used to serve it twice: first before the roast to fill you up and lessen your appetite for the expensive roast to follow, and then after the main course with jam on top in case you were still hungry. My other gran adhered to the delicious tradition of roasting the beef on a rack over the Yorkshire so that the meat juices dripped onto it. Yum.

Both these women were Scottish. So no surprise that it's a world favourite.

Prue Leith CBE

Toad in the Hole with Onion Gravy

Toad in the Hole turns Yorkshire Puddings into a filling meal with the addition of sausages. Just where the name Toad in the Hole comes from no-one really knows but originally the dish used spoonfuls of sausage meat, so the finished dish probably resembled toads peeping out of the batter?

The modern version uses a classic pork sausage but with so many great flavoured sausages available the versions of Toad in the Hole are endless.

Traditionally Toad in the Hole is made in a large square roasting tin which after cooking is sliced into hearty portions. Individual "Toads" can be made using a 12-hole muffin tin and cutting the sausages into thirds to fit each hole.

Serves 4

1 quantity of Yorkshire pudding batter (page 26)
1 tbsp vegetable oil
8 good quality, pork or flavoured sausages
1 quantity of Yorkshire pudding batter (see page 26), rested for minimum of 30 mins
1 tbsp lard, beef dripping or vegetable oil, for cooking

Heat the oven to 245°C/ 475°F/Gas 9 or as hot as possible.

Heat the oil in a frying pan, add the sausages and cook for 10 minutes until browned all over. Remove from the heat and keep to one side.

Drop the lard/dripping or oil into a 30cm x 24cm deep roasting tin. Place in the oven and heat until the fat is smoking hot. Remove from the oven and evenly arrange the sausages in the hot fat, taking extra care as the fat may splutter. Return to the oven for 5 minutes.

Once more remove the roasting tin from the oven. Slowly and

carefully pour the Yorkshire pudding batter into the hot fat and sausages, return to the oven and leave to cook for 30 minutes or until the pudding is golden and risen.

Serve with lashings of onion gravy (page 54) and fresh seasonal vegetables.

Irish Stew Filled Yorkshire Pudding

Serves 4

1 quantity of Yorkshire pudding batter (see page26)
2 tbsp vegetable oil
450g/1 lb mutton or lamb cutlets (bone removed) cut into
5cm chunks
1 kg/ 2 lb potatoes, peeled and cut into quarters
115g/4 oz onion, roughly chopped
115g/4 oz leeks, cleaned and finely sliced
170g/6 oz carrots, roughly chopped
750 ml/ 1 ¼ pints dark beef stock
2 or 3 cabbage leaves, thinly sliced (optional)
Salt and Pepper

Heat the oven to 180°C/350°F/ Gas 4

In a large frying pan heat half the oil to hot but not smoking. Add half the lamb pieces and brown all over.

Remove the lamb and place in a casserole dish, cover with half of the potatoes, onions, leeks and carrots.

Add the remaining oil to the frying pan, heat again then add the remaining lamb and brown all over. Add to the casserole and cover with the remaining vegetables.

Add the stock, cover with a tight fitting lid, cook in the oven for 1 hour.

Make the Yorkshire pudding batter according to the recipe and leave to rest while the Irish stew cooks.

Add the cabbage (if using) replace the lid and cook for another hour. Check from time to time to make sure the stock isn't reducing too much. If it is add a little boiling water. The meat and vegetables should always be covered by liquid. If the sauce is too runny at the end, cook a little longer with the lid removed, season with salt and pepper.

Heat the oven to the highest temperature possible. However, do not exceed 230°C/450°F/Gas 8 or the fat may burn.

Place a pea-sized piece of lard, dripping or ½tsp vegetable oil into 4 individual Yorkshire pudding, or 18cm Victoria sandwich tins and heat in the oven until the fat is smoking.

Give the batter another good whisk adding 2 tbsp of cold water and fill a third of the tin with batter and return quickly to the oven. Cook for 20 -25 minutes or until the pudding is golden and risen.

Place a Yorkshire pudding on a plate and fill with the Irish stew - delicious.

My mother made an excellent Yorkshire pudding. We used to eat it before the roast beef, all on its own, and it was light and crispy and delicious. Usually she made a big one in a baking tin, but later took to making individual ones in little tins. My father put gravy on his, and so I think did she, but at that age I hated gravy or anything soggy, so I liked it just as it was, straight from the oven. I don't know whether eating the Yorkshire pudding separately was a Yorkshire tradition, or whether it was just us. I have always avoided Yorkshire pudding in restaurants and cafes as it is never as good as hers and is usually covered in dubious gravy and vegetables.

In adult life I tried to make it myself but it was always heavy and soggy. My toad in the hole was worse than soggy, it was a culinary disaster, and everybody laughed at it. I gave up. Yorkshire pudding for me is nothing but a happy memory.

Dame Margaret Drabble

The Noble Roast Beef of Britain

When mighty Roast Beef was the Englishman's food,

It ennobled our brains and enriched our blood.

Our soldiers were brave and our courtiers were good

Oh! the Roast Beef of old England,

And old English Roast Beef!

'The Roast Beef of Old England'. An English patriotic ballad written by Henry Fielding for his play *The Grub-Street Opera*, first performed in 1731.

The British love of beef, and particularly for lunch on a Sunday, is nothing new. It is such a part of the national identity that even the French call us "rosbifs" (roast beefs) and the Yeoman of the Guard – the royal bodyguard – have been affectionately known as "beefeaters" since the 15th century. A telling observation is by Henri Misson, who staying in London in 1698, tells how "it is a common practice, even among People of Good Substance, to have a huge Piece of Roast-Beef on Sundays, of which they stuff until they can swallow no more, and eat the rest cold, without any other Victuals, the other six Days of the Week".

Startlingly, contrary to modern thinking about meat eating, in 1871 William Kitchener, author of *Apicius Redivivus or The Cook's Oracle*, recommended eating 3 kg (6lb) of meat each week as part of a healthy diet (he also recommended 2 kilos of bread and a pint of beer every day). Today in the UK we eat approximately 1.5 kg of meat each week – only 200g of which is beef – and some think even that is too much.

Kitchener also describes in the book how to roast "the noble sirloin of about fifteen pounds" before the fire for four hours for Sunday lunch. This method of hanging the meat on a spit or, in the 19th century, suspended from a bottle-jack – and certainly that size of a joint – demanded a sizeable fireplace. It would be to feed a large household not only on the Sunday but as cold cuts, stews and pies throughout the week.

The less well-off did not have the luxury of a large fireplace or the money for much meat, so the smaller weekly roast would be dropped off en-route to church at the bakers to be cooked in the cooling bread ovens – bread was not baked on a Sunday. With access for all to cook meat on a Sunday, the tradition of the British Sunday lunch began and still continues today.

Though meat is no longer roasted in front of the fire, but today is baked in the modern oven, we still cling on to the term Sunday 'roast'. On Sundays throughout the UK, pubs and restaurants are packed full for the roast dinner – some even serve the meal on other days of the week such is its popularity. But for many, cooking and serving Sunday lunch at home is the very heart of British food and cooking. It is the time for families or friends to get together and share good food. For the cook in the house, the Sunday roast with all the trimmings takes some putting together but the effort is worth it.

Though beef is the traditional meat for a Sunday roast, lamb, pork and chicken are equally as popular today.

Roast Beef and Gravy Recipe

The best joints for roast beef is a rib of beef, sirloin or fillet. Rib works well as usually it will be cooked on the bone. Keeping the bone in makes for a tastier piece of beef when cooked but both Sirloin and Fillet are very good. Choose beef which has:

A thick covering of fat to add flavour and prevent the joint from drying out during cooking.

Marbled. Marbling is small slivers of fat running through the flesh which again adds flavour and prevents drying out during cooking.

Dark in colour – meaning it has been hung well and mature.

To feed six people comfortably you will need

> Bone in - 2.5kg/5 ½ lb
> Boned - 1.5kg/ 3lb boned

Don't worry about buying too much. Cold roast beef makes great sandwiches or on a plate of cold cuts.

Ingredients

> 1 piece of beef (as above)
> 2 tsp dry English mustard powder
> 2 tsp plain flour
> Salt and pepper
> 1/2 glass red wine or port
> 500ml/1 pt meat or vegetable stock
> 1 tsp ice cold butter

Preheat the oven to 220°C/425°F /Gas 7

For even, accurate cooking the beef must be at room temperature.

Dust the surface of fat on the beef with the mixture of mustard and plain flour and season with salt and pepper.

Place the beef, fat side up in a roomy roasting tin. Place in the centre of the hot oven. After 20 minutes turn the oven down to 190°C/375°F/ Gas 5.

Cook as follows:

Rare 11 minutes per 450g/ lb
Medium 14 minutes per 450g/ lb
Well done 16 minutes per 450g/ lb

You can also cook using a thermometer inserted into the centre of the beef

60° C/140° F – rare
70° C/160F – medium
80° C/175 °F – well done

Baste the meat two or three times with the fat released during cooking.

Once cooked to your liking, remove the beef from the oven, keep the roasting tin to one side and rest the beef as follows.

Wrap the meat loosely in aluminum foil and put to one side. The fibres in meat tighten up during cooking and resting allows the fibres to relax, releasing some of the meat juices (great for the gravy) and results in a soft tender piece of meat. 20 minutes should be long enough but up to an hour is better.

Meanwhile make the gravy (see page 66):

Sunday lunch with roast beef and Yorkshire pudding is still at the very heart of British cooking. It is even better when served with roast potatoes and cauliflower cheese.

Gravy

The roasting pan contains all the meat juices from the roast which are an essential part of the gravy. Pour away any excess fat then place the roasting pan on the stove top over a high heat until the meat juices begin to bubble but not burn.

Pour in the red wine and scrape all the juices from the bottom of the pan, reduce to a sticky glaze. Do not leave the pan unattended as the reduction happens very quickly. Add the stock and stir well.

Strain the gravy through a fine sieve into a saucepan and reduce by one-third. Add any juices released from the resting beef. Bring back to the boil then reduce to a gentle simmer.

Add the butter in tiny pieces shaking the pan gently until all the butter is absorbed. Keep warm until needed.

Serve the beef and gravy with roast potatoes, fresh seasonal vegetables, cauliflower cheese, horseradish cream and, of course, Yorkshire puddings.

Yorkshire Pudding Boat Race

The Yorkshire Pudding Boat Race was first presented by The Shed in June 1999

Yorkshire pudding boats made from flour, water and eggs were coated in yacht varnish to prevent them sinking, and floated on Bob's Pond in Brawby, near Malton.

Poet Ian McMillan read the Yorkshire Pudding Boat Songs while saxophonist Snake Davis and the children of the Yorkshire Pudding Orchestra provided musical sound effects.

Perfect Roast Potatoes

Crisp, golden brown, roast potatoes straight from the oven – delicious. Duck or goose fat is easily available from good supermarkets or farm shops and brings a wonderful flavour to the potatoes. Don't worry if you can't find duck fat. Lard or vegetable oil if you prefer also works very well.

 If you have a large dinner to prepare and are pushed for time the potatoes can be half roasted the day before then reheated for 20 minutes in a hot oven.

Serves 4

lb /500g floury potatoes, peeled,
Desirée or King Edward's are good
4 tbsp goose or duck fat, lard or vegetable oil
Salt and pepper

Preheat the oven to 220°C/425°F/Gas 7

Cut the potatoes into even-sized pieces. And rinse under cold water.

Place the potatoes in a saucepan, cover with cold water, add a sprinkle of salt and bring to the boil. Once boiling lower the heat and simmer for 10 minutes.

Drain the potatoes in a colander. Gently shake the colander to fluff the outside of the potatoes.

Heat the fat or oil in a roasting tin until very hot but not burning. Carefully tip the potatoes into the hot fat. Using a tablespoon coat each potato with the hot fat in the tin, this will help prevent the potatoes from sticking.

Return the roasting tin to the hot oven and roast until golden brown and crisp turning the potatoes from time to time approx 45 minutes.

Serve immediately.

Cauliflower Cheese

Cauliflower is an essential side dish for a traditional Roast Beef Sunday Lunch. Cauliflower cheese is quick and easy to prepare and makes the most of British cauliflowers which are not only cheap but available almost year round.

1 medium cauliflower (approx 450g/1 lb)
55g /2 oz butter
55g / 2 oz plain flour
1 level tsp mustard powder (optional)
Large pinch salt
460 ml /1 pint milk
55g/ 2 oz cheddar cheese or similar, grated plus extra for sprinkling on top
Freshly ground pepper

Heat the oven to 200°C/395°F/Gas 7

Remove the green outer leaves from the cauliflower and steam whole over a pan of boiling water for 10 minutes. Remove the cauliflower from the heat and leave to cool.

Place the butter and flour into a large saucepan. Over a low heat stir the butter and flour until the butter has melted and the flour is incorporated. Add the salt and mustard powder and continue cooking stirring constantly for 2 minutes.

Turn the heat up to medium and add the milk in one go and whisk furiously until a smooth sauce is formed. Continue stirring until the sauce is thickened and glossy (about 5 minutes). If the sauce is very thick add a little more milk, the sauce should be thick but still runny. Add the grated cheese and stir until melted. Remove from the heat.

Break the cauliflower florets from the thick, central stalk taking care not to break it into tiny pieces. Place the florets in a baking dish large enough to hold all the florets in one layer.

Pour the thickened cheese sauce over the cauliflower ensuring all the florets are covered. Sprinkle with grated cheese and a good twist of black pepper.

Bake in the hot oven until the sauce is bubbling and golden brown on the top, approx 30 minutes.

Horseradish Cream

Horseradish cream is a lovely sauce to serve with roast beef, adding a welcome piquancy to the dish. Make before starting to cook the beef, as this allows the flavour to develop.

    2 tbsp freshly, grated horseradish
    350 ml/12 fl oz crème fraîche
    Pinch mustard powder
    1 tsp lemon juice
    Salt and white pepper

In a small bowl mix together all the ingredients except the salt and pepper. You should have a thick cream. Cover with cling film until ready to serve. Just before serving check the seasoning and add salt and pepper to taste.

Rhubarb Crumble with Custard

No Sunday lunch is complete without a traditional British pudding – not a Yorkshire one this time.

Serves 4

Crumble:

12 stalks of fresh rhubarb, washed, cut into 5cm/2" pieces

4 tbsp water

8 tbsp caster sugar

115g / 4 oz butter, cut into small cubes

115g/ 4 oz Demerara sugar

170g/ 6 oz plain flour

Custard:

150ml / 5 fl oz milk

250ml/ 8 ½ fl oz double cream

1 vanilla pod, split and seeds removed

55g/ 2 oz caster sugar

6 large egg yolks

Heat the oven to 180°C/350°F/Gas 4.

Place the rhubarb and water into a 4 cm/1 ½" deep ovenproof dish and sprinkle the sugar over.

In a baking bowl rub the butter, sugar and flour together until it resembles fine sand, then sprinkle over the rhubarb.

Bake in the oven for approx 45 mins - 1 hour until golden brown on the top and the fruit is bubbling.

Meanwhile make the custard. In a heavy bottomed saucepan place the milk, cream, vanilla pod (not the seeds) and one tsp of the sugar. Bring to a gentle simmer, once simmering turn the heat to its lowest and keep the milk mixture warm, but not hot.

In a large heatproof bowl, place the sugar and the egg yolks and with a hand whisk, whisk until light, creamy and pale in colour.

Slowly, whilst still whisking, pour the warmed milk into the egg mixture.

Strain the custard sauce through a fine sieve back into the saucepan and add the seeds from the vanilla pod. Over a low heat, stir the custard continuously and gradually the custard will thicken. Do not speed this process up or you run the risk of the sauce curdling, and even worse burning.

Finally, once thickened, remove from the heat and pass through a sieve again into a warmed serving jug.

Serve over the hot crumble.

Yorkshire Pudding Walk

In Marsden near Huddersfield, the Annual Yorkshire Pudding Walk takes place on Yorkshire Day – August 1st. The eight-mile walk ends with a three-course meal, including Yorkshire Puddings.

Yorkshire Puddings filled with Wild Mushrooms

By Ghislaine Miller – Owner-Baker, Laine's Cornerstone Kitchen, Florida, USA

There is a big interest in the United States for Yorkshire puddings. They may call them popovers but they are essentially the same. I was sent this recipe after Ghislaine read about Yorkshire pudding on the About British Food website. It is an inventive way of serving the puddings to vegetarians, but also great for committed carnivores.

1 quantity of Yorkshire pudding batter (page26) with 1 tsp dried or 2 tsp fresh thyme, 1 ½ tsp dried or 2 tsp fresh parsley and 1 tsp dried sage mixed into the batter.

For the Filling:

120 ml/ 4 fl oz extra virgin olive oil

2 tbsp butter

1 kg/2 1b mixed wild mushrooms, brushed clean and sliced thickly

or, 500g/1 lb thick sliced button mushrooms and 500g/ 1lb wild mushrooms

4 garlic clove, finely chopped

1 ½ tsp dried sage

½ tsp dried red pepper flakes (optional)

1 tsp salt

½ tsp freshly ground black pepper to taste

115g/4 oz finely grated cheese, Parmesan or Pecorino Romano

Cook the Yorkshire puddings as per the recipe using a four-hole Yorkshire pudding tin (4 x 5cm/2in).

While the puddings are cooking, prepare the mushroom filling.

Heat the olive oil in a large frying pan over medium high heat. Add the mushrooms and butter, reduce heat to medium until they are tender, stirring frequently – about 10 minutes.

Add the garlic, sage, salt, pepper and dried red pepper flakes if using. Keep stirring and cook for additional 2 to 3 minutes. Adjust seasoning to taste.

Place in prepared Yorkshire pudding, garnish with cheese and serve immediately.

What can one say about the great Yorkshire pudding that has not been said already?

Our grandparents could turn out the perfect "Yorkshire" using the old, coal-fed, black-leaded fire grates and side ovens. Then our parents did the same, using the more modern cookers, with just the four controls: high, medium, low and off.

No mention in those days of "centigrade this" and "centigrade that"; as a temperature, just "bang some coal on the fire" or "turn it up to high" was all that was needed.

Lo and behold, the perfect Yorkshire to go with the Sunday joint.

Sunday lunch without Yorkshire pudding is not a Sunday lunch.

The texture and crispness when the knife goes in and the gravy starts to run around, there is no better start to a meal than this.

Served as a starter or with the meal it was, and still is, always the first item you aim for on your plate.

Dickie Bird

Caramelised Apple Yorkshire Pudding

Ingredients:

> 1 tbsp butter
>
> 1 tbsp golden caster sugar
>
> 1 Bramley apple, peeled, quartered and core removed.
>
> 1 quantity of Yorkshire Pudding batter (see page 26)
>
> Vanilla ice cream to serve

Method:

Make the Yorkshire pudding batter according to the recipe and leave to rest for at least 30 minutes up to several hours.

Melt the butter in a large frying pan over a medium high heat. Add the sugar, stir until it dissolves then turn up the heat and boil the butter and sugar for 3 – 4 minutes or until golden brown. Do not stir during this time, simply shake the pan once or twice to prevent the sauce from sticking.

Meanwhile, slice the apple quarters to thickness of £1 coin. Once the sauce is cooked lower the heat back to medium and add the apple slices in a single layer in the pan. Cook for 2 - 3 minutes on one side, turn the slices over and cook for another 2 – 3 minutes. The apple slices should be golden and sticky. Remove from the heat and keep to one side.

Heat the oven to the highest temperature possible. However, do not exceed 230°C/450°F/Gas 8 or the fat may burn.

Place a pea-sized piece of lard, dripping or ½tsp vegetable oil into 4 individual Yorkshire pudding, or 18cm Victoria sandwich tins and heat in the oven until the fat is smoking.

Remove the tins from the oven, divide the apple slices between the tins.

Give the batter another good whisk adding 2 tbsp of cold water and fill a third of the tin with batter and return quickly to the oven. Cook for 20 – 25 minutes or until the pudding is risen and golden.

Serve immediately with vanilla ice cream.

Yorkshire Pond Puddings

by food writer Sarah Beattie

Nothing like Sussex Pond Pudding – this is a Double Chocolate Yorkshire Pudding, deep dark and muddy! Serve with thick cream and some hot strawberries, stir fried in butter and vanilla sugar.

    115g/4 oz plain flour
    15g/ ½ oz cocoa powder
    1 tbsp caster sugar
    1 large + 1 medium egg
    300ml / 10 fl oz semi-skimmed milk
    Light vegetable oil
    A handful of chocolate chips

Proceed as for classic Yorkshire sifting the flour, cocoa and sugar together and beating in the egg and milk.

Preheat a Yorkshire pudding tin with a little vegetable oil in each cup. When hot, pour in the batter and add 4 or 5 chocolate chips in the centre of each pudding.

Bake until risen and firm (about 12 minutes). Serve immediately, dusted with icing sugar.

Raspberry Vinegar

by food writer Maxine Clark

Makes about 725ml of vinegar

225g/ ½ lb fresh or frozen raspberries, thawed
285ml/10 fl oz cider or wine vinegar
Caster sugar

To make the vinegar, place the raspberries in a non-corrosive jug or jar and cover with the vinegar.

Leave in a cool place for 5 days (2 at the least), shaking occasionally.

Strain (without crushing) into a measuring jug and discard the now-floppy raspberries.

Measure the liquid and pour into a saucepan, adding 350g sugar per 600ml of liquid. Bring slowly to the boil to dissolve the sugar, then boil for 2-3 minutes until lightly syrupy.

Pour into warm sterilised bottles and seal.

The World Black Pudding Throwing Championship

Nowhere is the ancient rivalry between Lancashire and Yorkshire displayed more than at the annual Black Pudding Throwing Contest in the small town of Ramsbottom in Lancashire.

Contestants throw black puddings at a stack of Yorkshire puddings piled onto a twenty-foot plinth. Each is allowed to throw three 6 oz Bury puddings. Whoever fells the most Yorkshire puddings is the winner.

In the late 1990's I had been a regular on ITV's This Morning with Richard and Judy for about five years and I eventually agreed to make Yorkshire pudding live on TV. A bit like a soufflé, it needs good timing for the cameras to show the real beauty of a five-inch tall Yorkshire!

So we prepared a mix, my Grandma Riley's recipe, a cup of flour, a cup of eggs, a cup of milk and water, a pinch of salt and a splash of malt vinegar (don't ask why, I don't know, but it works)!

We were due to be on screen at 10.55am and had to finish on the dot at 11am for the news. The Yorkshires were put in the top oven, we had two (posh huh in those days) at full heat at 10.25 and we went live. Unfortunately as was often the case, the item before mine overran and so we went on air at 10.56 or so and had to rush.

I made the batter, then put the puds into a full heat in the bottom oven, closed the door and took out the ones from the top oven. Sadly whoever had put the puddings in the top oven had put the grill on so that direct heat was beaming down on the Yorkshires stopping them from rising and in fact making them like bread cakes – how red was my face?

Happily Richard and Judy allowed me to show the ones from the bottom oven as soon as they came out and magnificent they were – my reputation remains intact!

Brian Turner (celebrity chef and Yorkshireman)

Yorkshire Puddings and Special Diets

No need to pass on the puddings because of a dietary restriction. These recipes with give you a decent Yorkshire pudding.

Gluten Free Yorkshire Puddings

> 2 large eggs
> Pinch salt
> 300ml/ 10 fl oz milk
> 75g/3 oz gluten free flour
> 55g/2 oz cornflour
> 1 tsp Xanthan gum
> 25g/1 oz lard, dripping, or vegetable oil

Heat oven to 220°C/425°F/Gas 7

In a large mixing bowl, beat the eggs, salt and milk together. In a separate bowl, mix the flour, cornflour and gum.

Beating constantly, slowly add the flour mixture to the egg and milk and continue to beat until a smooth, lump-free batter is formed.

Put a pea-sized piece of lard, dripping or ½ tsp oil into a tart, muffin tray or 25cm x 30cm oven dish.

Place the tray or dish into the hot oven until the fat is smoking hot.

Fill each cavity by one-third and return to the oven. Cook until puffed up and golden, 25 – 30 minutes.

Kosher Yorkshire Pudding

Serves 6

4 large, fresh eggs, measured in a jug
Equal quantity of soya milk to eggs
Equal quantity of plain flour to eggs
Pinch of salt
Lard, beef dripping or vegetable oil for cooking

Heat the oven to the highest temperature possible. However, do not exceed 230°C/450 °F/Gas 8 or the fat may burn.

Pour the eggs and milk into a large mixing bowl and add the pinch of salt. Whisk thoroughly with an electric or hand-whisk until foamy. Leave to stand for about 10 minutes to allow the bubbles to subside.

Sieve the flour into the milk and egg mixture and beat again using an electric or hand-whisk to create a lump free batter resembling thick cream. Finally pass the batter through a sieve into another bowl of jug.

Leave the batter to rest in the kitchen for a minimum of 30 minutes up to a couple of hours, the longer the better.

Place ½ tsp vegetable oil in a Yorkshire pudding tin (4 x 5cm/2in hole tin) or 12-hole muffin tin and heat in the oven until the fat is smoking.

Give the batter another good whisk adding 2 tbsp of cold water and fill a third of each section of the tin with batter and return quickly to the oven.

Leave to cook until risen and golden brown, approx 20 minutes. Repeat the last step again without adding any water until all the batter is used up.

Recommended Suppliers

Meat
Paganum Online Farmers Market, Yorkshire
http://www.paganum.co.uk

Lishman's
25 Leeds Road, Ilkley, West Yorkshire, LS29 8DP
Telephone: 01943 609436
http://www.lishmansonline.co.uk

Butchery, Bakery, Fresh Fruit & Veg, Dairy & Eggs
Fodder
Great Yorkshire Showground, Harrogate, HG2 8NZ
Telephone: 01423 546 111
http://www.fodderweb.co.uk

Weeton's
23-24 West Park, Harrogate, HG1 1BJ
Telephone: 01423 507 100

Oils and Vinegars
Womersley Foods
Normanton, West Yorkshire
http://www.womersleyfoods.co.uk
For details of where to buy products call 44 (0)1924 895856
or email admin@womersleyfoods.co.uk

Kitchenware
Lakeland
48 stores across the UK, or online
http://www.lakeland.co.uk